A LIFETIME OF FLOWERS

Jenny Brook

A LIFETIME
OF FLOWERS

Jenny Brook

Watercolour Illustrations by the Author

PENTLAND BOOKS

British cataloguing in publication data.
A catalogue record for this book is
available from the British Library.

Poetry quotations are from *Wild Flowers* by Anne Pratt (London, 1893).

Published in 2001 by
Pentland Books
Hutton Close
Bishop Auckland
Durham.

ISBN: 1 85821 895 0

Typeset, printed and bound by
Lintons Printers
Crook
County Durham

*This book has been written and illustrated in memory of
my dear brother, who started me on the road to
'a lifetime of flowers' a long time ago.*

FOREWORD

Here is a book that will transport you to the wonders of the pure natural world. A world, that as a painter of nature, I have lived with and appreciated all my life. I recognise in Jenny's enthusiastic words the love of nature that comes from early influences and stays with one all one's life. That love is a constant source of solace and pleasure that no one can deny.

Throughout this book you will be introduced again to flowers in a way that will stop you in your tracks. You may have thought you knew something about flowers, wild and garden, but this will reopen your eyes to their beauty and the pleasure they can give.

The beautiful illustrations alone will be a constant source of delight and a means of identifying the different species.

It will bring back memories of childhood times when there seemed to be more flowers around. The flowers are still there but perhaps in less abundance in some places. I am sure after reading this book you will soon be out in the countryside again to look, no, observe these wonders of nature. I will be taking a magnifying glass, a camera, my sketchbook and paints to restart 'collecting' and enjoying the sheer beauty of these unique plants, as I am sure you will be too.

Alan Oliver - International Artist.

AUTHOR'S NOTE

As some of the plants described in this book are poisonous, it is advisable for readers to seek professional opinion from a trained herbal practitioner before attempting to use any of the remedies to treat themselves.

ACKNOWLEDGEMENTS

My thanks to my daughter Pauline and her husband Barry for sharing my enthusiasm in producing this book.

To my son Gerald and his wife Susan for their interest shown in each stage of my writing.

I thank my friends Hazel and June for their kind assistance and encouragement.

CONTENTS

LIST OF ILLUSTRATIONS

INTRODUCTION
My early life with flowers

For as long as I can remember my life has revolved around flowers.

I was born in Yorkshire opposite an extensive natural park, which, as children, we visited almost every day, to play amongst the massive collection of rhododendron bushes, where almost every colour you can think of was represented in their blooms. This indeed was a delightful spectacle and I am sure is the reason for my favourite flower being the rhododendron.

When I was six or seven years old, I would go along with my brother, four years my senior, to the park after school. We made our way through the rhododendrons to the wood which lay beyond. Unlike the present day, this was quite a safe thing for children to do. Together we would wander around looking out for the many wild flowers that grew there. We knew all their habitats and the season when they appeared. In the spring the bluebell, the delicate wood anenome, the primrose and the celandine would all be showing their faces.

Situated in the park was a Natural History Museum which we visited frequently, making friends with the lady caretaker. I thought Mrs Hart was a very old lady at the time, but, on reflection, I am sure she certainly was not as old as a little child like myself believed her to be. Just inside the main entrance to the Museum was a long table on which stood several glass jars filled with clean water, all labelled with the names of wild flowers which grew in the wood. At least twice a week, after collecting our flower specimens, we took them along to the Museum, and Mrs Hart helped us to identify them and place them into the correct containers. It did not take long for us to recognise the flowers for ourselves and collecting soon became an exciting hobby.

At the entrance to the park, we had to make a detour to a bank alongside the railway bridge to locate two of the earliest flowers of the year. In the months of February and March we would find dog's mercury and the yellow coltsfoot growing there - they never failed us!

When we were a little older and became more adventurous, during the school holidays our parents allowed us to travel a good bit further to other countryside locations. Taking a picnic, we would go down the country lanes diligently searching the hedgerows. At different seasons we would find traveller's joy, wild rose, cuckoo pint and the woody nightshade and others.

On then into the meadow where field varieties grew in great profusion. There would be red sorrel, buttercups, common daisies, bird's-foot trefoil, the clovers and many more. Skirting the cornfields we would find ox-eye daisies, corn poppies and blue cornflowers making a very pretty picture amongst the corn.

Lastly to the woodland, collecting some of the prettiest specimens ever to be seen. In spring were the primroses and violets growing in great abundance, and in summer months the stately form of one of the most handsome plants, the deep pink/purple foxglove.

We returned home, very tired but very happy, having collected lots of new exciting flowers, which were then rolled in long pieces of newspaper to keep them upright. They were placed in a bucket of deep water and taken to the dark cellar until the following day. Our specimens then having revived and looking very fresh, they were ready to be identified and named.

Imagine our delight when, at about this time, we were given some books about wild flowers by an elderly couple. The books, now well over one hundred years old and still in my possession, were a wonderful gift and became our Wild Flower Bible. We spent many hours and had lots of fun, reading and identifying our flowers and learning about their uses in earlier times.

Even though my brother still had an interest in the plants, when he obtained a place in Grammar School he had very little time to pursue the hobby in a practical way but he still showed enthusiasm for what I did. I continued to collect wild flowers whenever I could and moved on to learn the art of pressing specimens and mounting them in exercise books. I filled books each season for several years, learning more and more about flowers.

All too soon childhood was passing us by. I gained an Art Scholarship and consequently was accepted into art school for a two-and-a-half-years' course where I always used lots of flower designs in my work.

PART I

FLOWERS AND MY FAMILY

Years later, when our two children were quite young, the interest in wild-flower hunting was revived.

Nearly every weekend, as a family, we travelled to various parts of the countryside spending many hours in our quest for flowers. The children were always very excited when we came across something new. Visiting the local library about this time, I found a book entitled *Flowers of the Field* written by the Reverend C. A. Johns, which I borrowed and renewed over and over again. This was a fantastic find, helping greatly with the identification of the plants. When the children were in bed, I spent much of my time reading, learning and following the explanation of the terms, parts of the flowers, and the many tribes and classes to which the flowers belonged. I never did master the Latin names! Only this last year, by sheer good fortune, my daughter found this very same book in a secondhand book shop. Needless to say she bought it and presented it to me. I was so delighted to have it for myself. *Flowers of the Field* was written over a hundred years ago. It brought back such happy memories to me.

When our little daughter was at junior school, her class teacher arranged a nature competition. This was quite uncanny. He asked the children to collect wild flowers, as many as possible, and take them to school every Monday morning. They were asked to name the flowers and even spell the names. The competition ran from spring to autumn. This was a real challenge, a great thrill for our young daughter, and an incentive to get more involved in collecting.

Every Saturday the family spent the day collecting from both old and new localities, bringing home lots of specimens at the end of the afternoon. During the weekend we identified and named the plants and had a spelling lesson. Each Monday morning our daughter took them to school and presented them to the teacher complete with the necessary information. She never tired of doing this throughout the months of the contest, and at the close of it she was the prizewinner, having collected one hundred and forty-eight specimens.

Her teacher would sometimes dispute her identification and ask her how she knew what the plants were. Her answer was 'because Mummy says so'. Consequently I received a letter from him, asking me when I was going to write a book on 'Collecting Wild Flowers'.

Flowers are more abundant in some parts of the country than others. When we moved from our native Yorkshire to the East Midlands and found our way around this alien place, we occasionally came across a new variety we had never seen before.

Have you ever looked very closely into a wild flower? Some people would dismiss them all as weeds. But look carefully and study the formation, structure and design. You will marvel at what you see and wonder at such delicacy and exquisite beauty!

~ WILD FLOWERS ~

Fig. 1
RANSOM

Fig. 2 COLTSFOOT - This is one of the earliest of the spring flowers, often blooming in March. It grows on clayey banks and also on barren plains where few other plants are found. The yellow flowers appear long before the leaves, which are large, handsome and spreading. The under-surface of the leaf of the coltsfoot is covered with a thick, cottony down, which in early times was often used for tinder when that substance was in demand. These leaves were very much used medicinally as an infusion for coughs, and people smoked them like tobacco.

The scientific name for the genus is derived from *tussis*, meaning 'cough'. The flowers bloom from the beginning of March until the end of April, giving quite a yellow hue to the land where they abound.

Fig. 3 PRIMROSE - The primrose is the first of the woodland flowers, sometimes blooming as early as February as spring approaches. It has been commonly described as sulphur-coloured, but an early botanist remarked that 'the colour of the flower is so peculiar as to have a name of its own - artists using that "primrose colour" as a delicate green'. The flower is in full bloom from February until May in woods and on banks. It is left untouched by cattle, not one of the primrose family being relished by any animal with the exception of the pig.

In early times country people gathered the petals and made them into ointment but, although highly prized in villages, it was not a powerful remedy.

There are other wild plants included in the genus, the oxlip and the cowslip and also the bird's-eye primrose, a very lovely flower of pale lilac-pink. The latter plant is a summer flower appearing on the mountainous pastures of the north of England in July.

Fig. 4 SWEET VIOLET - The sweet purple violets are among the first favourites of all spring flowers. We find them in March but they are more abundant in April. They grow in the woods and on the wayside. A poet's description says:

> *'There purple violets lurk,*
> *with all the lovely children of the shade.'*

In earlier times violet flower petals were boiled and mixed with sugar and used in confectionery. The scent is used in perfume and is an emblem of modesty. There are six other species of violet including the little pansy or heart's-ease of the fields.

Fig. 5 WOOD ANENOME - How lovely are the woodlands during the months of April and May, with the song of the birds, the rustle of the new leaves on the trees and the sweet scents of the spring flowers. But not one of the blossoms is more beautiful than that of the wood anenome, or windflower as it is called in some parts of the country. Its white petals are so delicate, it is hard to believe that it will be unharmed by the strong breezes. In some woods the wood anenome is quite plentiful, its seeds being wafted around in the wind, its tough roots creeping underneath the surface of the soil.

There are other wild varieties blooming in the spring but none so common as the one shown in the illustration.

Fig. 6 LESSER CELANDINE - Who does not welcome one of our brightest early flowers, studding every bank and meadow with its numerous glossy yellow flowers? The lesser celandine or pilewort, with its glittering golden stars, gleams among the grass from March until the end of May.

> *'The vernal pileworts'globe unfold*
> *Its star-like disc of burnished gold,*
> *Starlike in seeming form, from far*
> *It shines too like a glistening star.'*

The flower is a true lover of sunshine, opening only on bright days. The celandine closes its petals from five o'clock in the evening until nine next morning.

Although wild-flower lovers greet the celandine with great pleasure, the farmer would gladly eradicate it from his land. It has acrimonious properties and, because of this, is left untouched by cattle. Although the plant was used for medicinal purposes, it is said to injure other plants growing near to it.

Fig. 7 BLUEBELL or WILD HYACINTH - Most people who have wandered through the woods in the months of April or May know the bluebell or wild hyacinth. Some years ago, woodlands in the spring would be carpeted with the beautiful blue flowers. Sadly today, however, this is no longer true. Also at this time, the may-blossom is starting to bloom, the wood anenomes are fading, the primroses have almost departed, and the violets are becoming more rare.

The wild hyacinth is plentiful. The root is round and full of a poisonous sticky juice, in fact every part of the plant gives out more or less of this juice if it is bruised. Although the root or bulb is unfit for food and today is useless to us, in former times it was very prized. In the days when stiff ruffs and cuffs were worn, the juice was made into starch and used to stiffen linen. The bookbinder used the juice as a glue to fasten together the book covers. The flowers have a slight scent, but the real charm of the bluebells is their beauty and colour. Their early appearance seems to say:

> *'The winter is past, the rain is over and gone,*
> *The flowers appear on the earth and the time*
> *for the singing of the birds has come.'*

Fig. 8 RED DEAD NETTLE - Hardly before we have begun to hunt for the early wild flowers, the blossom of this dead nettle will be noticed on the hedge bank. Winter has few wild flowers but this dead nettle, with its rather dull reddish-purple blooms, can be observed as early as February, if the day is sunny. It is found in all parts of Britain and is in bloom until September. The upper leaves occasionally have a purplish tinge and are covered with silky hairs.

In former days it was in great esteem among country people as a healing remedy for wounds. The odour of the species is not agreeable, but many other useful plants such as sage and different kinds of mint belong to the same family. They all have square stems, opposite leaves and two-lipped blossoms.

Fig. 9 WHITE DEAD NETTLE - The foliage of this plant bears a strong resemblance to that of the stinging nettle, but is devoid of the stinging properties, hence its name 'dead'. The white dead nettle is one of the earliest spring flowers and can be seen almost any time during summer, most abundantly in June and July. It abounds on field borders, hedges and waste places.

It is refused by cattle, but, as with other nettle species, in early days it was boiled as a vegetable. At the base of the flower lies a store of honey for the bee, butterfly and other insects.

A clergyman described the nettle family as follows:

> *'And there, with whorls encircling graced*
> *Of white, and purple tinted red,*
> *The harmless nettle's helmet head;*
> *Less apt with fragrance to delight*
> *The smell, than please the envious sight.'*

Fig. 10 DANDELION - Many thousands of these golden flowers gleam in the springtime in the meadows and on the banks from April right through the chilly frosts in late autumn.
In former times the leaves of the dandelion were sold to be eaten in salads. In modern times the roots of the plant are ground and mixed with coffee, hence the beverage 'Dandelion Coffee'. When the roots are sliced and boiled, the decoction is valuable as a remedy for long-standing liver complaints. The liquid is an excellent tonic and will also clear the complexion, possibly far more than any cosmetic.
The deeply-cut leaves of the dandelion grow direct from the root and the flower stalk is tubular, bearing a single flower. The ball of down which succeeds the flower is quite remarkable and was given the name 'clock'. It is said, if the down flies from the stalk when there is no wind, it is a sign of rain. The abundance of this seed renders the plant difficult to control, as every inch of root will form thousands of buds and fibres, therefore producing a great amount of new plants.

Fig. 11 GERMANDER SPEEDWELL - This flower is often confused with the forget-me-not, but it is one of the numerous family of the speedwells.

The germander speedwell is known by its peculiarity of the lower segment of its four petals being narrower than the rest. There are no less than eighteen wild varieties of the species, all of a striking blue hue, the germander being the largest of the family and consequently the most conspicuous, as it lies amongst the bright spring grass in Maytime. Some of the tribe bloom earlier still.

The speedwells are not now considered to possess medical properties but were once believed to yield valuable remedies.

Fig. 12 CUCKOO PINT - In different parts of the country, this plant has been given various names and is known as 'lords and ladies', 'cuckoo pint', 'wild arum' and others. There is no possibility of confusion with other species. The plant is common in our English hedgerows and is in flower during April and May.

The complete flowerhead is a fly-trap. The flies are attracted by the smell which is emitted from the club-shaped broad blade. The flies slip down the smooth sides of the column into the inside of the trap where stiff hairs prevent them from escaping. At the bottom of the blade there is water containing nectar. However, after the flowers have been pollinated, the blade or spathe shrivels and the flies go free.

The large shining leaves are marked with dark green patches, and in winter thick clusters of bright orange berries surround the stem.

The root was much used during the reign of Queen Elizabeth I to stiffen linen for ladies' garments which, being so thin, needed a strong starch to improve the quality of the material. This starch, however, badly irritated the hands of those who had to use it.

Fig. 13 GORSE or FURZE - The common gorse begins to bloom in May but the golden flowers can be seen even when the cold winds of autumn have withered almost all other flowers, so we are accustomed to look upon the common furze as one of the hardiest of plants. The flowers bloom upon the bleakest common and bear well the strong sea breezes. The gorse is not considered to be a profitable plant yet is useful to birds, butterflies and other living creatures. The roots are sometimes used for binding loose soil and the plant is often grown on hillsides for this purpose.

Fig. 14 COMMON BROOM - Far away over many heathlands we see the bright golden blossoms of the broom. If we stray among them on a sunny day in July, we may see the dark brown pods opening to let out their ripe seeds. The blossoms invite butterflies to linger around them and the bees keep a perpetual humming near them.

In former times the bark of the broom was steeped in water and the fibres used instead of flax. The twigs and branches were used for tanning leather and the young boughs made into brooms, hence its name.

The plant can grow to a height of twelve feet. It is quite an ornamental plant, for when the flowers have withered, its dark green leaves and twigs remain. Wordsworth describes it well:

> *'Am I not*
> *In truth a favoured plant?*
> *On me such bounty summer showers,*
> *That I am covered o'er with flowers,*
> *And when the frost is in the sky*
> *My branches are so fresh and gay*
> *That you might look on me and say -*
> *This plant can never die.'*

Fig. 15 GREATER STITCHWORT - This wayside and woodland flower is such a delight to see in the month of May. It has been named 'satin flower' owing to the pearly appearance of its white flowers.

The stitchwort is of the chickweed tribe and has many different varieties. Chickweed is given to caged birds, and young buds and seeds form a valuable supply of food to our wild birds throughout the greater part of the year.

Fig. 16 CUCKOO FLOWER - This wild plant, which is plentiful in moist meadows, is also known as the 'ladies smock' and blooms in the month of May. Before the sun has fully whitened it, it is a delicate lilac colour and is sometimes found with double flowers. The root leaves have a different formation to those of the stem, which are roundish and slightly toothed.

The foliage is pungent and was formerly used in salads but has not the pleasant flavour of the watercress, which is often its companion on the borders of a stream.

Fig. 17 WOOD SORREL - The leaves of the wood sorrel produce a strong acid which resembles that of the lemon. Hence the leaf is very pleasant in flavour and used in salads, and also a medicinal drink is made from the juice. The plant blooms in May and is abundant in woods and shady places. The leaves are extremely sensitive, closing during darkness or at the approach to a storm.

Some of the early religious painters of Italy, such as Fra Angelico, introduced the wood sorrel into their pictures. The triple leaf and the purple stained white flower gave rise to a strange understanding that this was the shamrock chosen by St Patrick to illustrate the doctrine of the Trinity.

Fig. 18 BUTTERCUP - In the month of May, these bright yellow buttercups are scattered in their thousands over the damp grassy meadows, contrasting well with their companions, the silvery white daisies.

The buttercup belongs to the extensive crowsfoot tribe. The flowers are showy, and all the British species are herbaceous, with leaves much divided. Most of them possess acrid and poisonous properties if taken into the stomach and can cause blisters if applied to the skin. All the crowsfoot species contain much acidity and are therefore disliked by cattle on this account.

There are fifteen different varieties of the crowsfoot family. Old writers called them by various names such as 'gold cup', 'cuckoo buds' and 'May buds'.

Fig. 19 COMMON DAISY - This is the only British species and too well known and admired to need description. The daisy flowers all the year round.

English and Scottish poets have sung its praises through many decades, Wordsworth describing it as 'the poet's darling'. Like the wind the daisy comes to almost every field, and in the north it is called 'bairnswort' because it is so loved by children. When in Brazil, the late botanist Gardner wrote his thoughts of the daisy:

> 'I wander alone, and often look
> For the primrose bank by the rippling brook;
> Which, waken'd to life by vernal beams
> An emblem of youth and beauty seems;
> And I ask where the violet and daisy grow
> But a breeze-born voice, in whispering low,
> Swept from the North o'er southern seas
> Tells me I'm far from the land of these.'

Fig. 20 HONEYSUCKLE - The honeysuckle has been the emblem of longstanding affection. When it winds itself around a bush or shrub, it entwines with such a strong grip that the mark can usually be seen on the branch which supports it.

There are several varieties growing in our gardens, some blossoming early, some with very bright colours, but none with such a sweet fragrance as the hedgerow honeysuckle. The pale-yellow part of the flower appears to burst open at dusk. At the base of the long tubular petal lies the honey, which, though the bee may not reach it, is extracted by the hawk-moth, with its long proboscis, so fertilising the plant. The herbalist Gerard tells us that if the flowers are steeped in oil and set in the sun, they will warm up a body which has grown very cold.

Other names have been given to the honeysuckle of the countryside, 'woodbine' and 'goat leaf', the latter being so named because the goat relishes the leaves. The plant climbs over craggy and inaccessible places, as is the habit of the goat. The honeysuckle always endeavours to follow the same course as the sun, twisting and turning itself from left to right. In the months of September and October, clusters of attractive dark red berries replace the flowers, adding to the beauty of the autumn woods and hedges.

There are two other species of wild honeysuckle, the perfoliate honeysuckle and the fly-honeysuckle, but these are rarely found in Britain.

Fig. 21 BLADDER CAMPION - This plant, which starts to flower in June, is quite common in most parts of the country, although in a few districts it is quite a rarity. It occasionally grows in weedy dry places but is more frequently seen by the roadsides.

It is distinguished from other species by the bladder-like flower cup which is veined by a network design. The plant has quite a strong perfume, secretes abundant nectar in its flowers and is pollinated by moths. Sometimes the secretions are so profuse that the stems and leaves are seen to be covered with small black insects which they have attracted and imprisoned. The young shoots have an odour and flavour of green peas and, although quite bitter in taste, they were formerly lightly boiled and eaten as a vegetable.

Fig. 22   RED and WHITE CAMPION - These are handsome wild flowers. The red campions flourish on the hedge banks or green meadows. The absence of fragrance is compensated for by their beauty in May and June. They usually attain a height of one or two feet.

In all respects the white campion resembles the above, except for its colour and its sweet evening fragrance. Petals of both varieties are deeply cleft into two, the inflated calyx is veined and the stems and leaves are markedly hairy.

Fig. 23 COMMON BORAGE - This species is mainly found on waste ground, rubbish dumps and near houses. It is particularly attractive to bees and it is said they derive more nourishment from borage than any other flower. The brilliant blue petals are very handsome, opening to the sun in June, and may be distinguished from other plants by their prominent black anthers.

The juice has the smell and flavour of cucumber and was an ingredient of a beverage called 'cad tankard'. In former years, the young leaves were boiled or used in salads, even though their flavour was anything but agreeable. The flowers steeped in wine were found to be very invigorating, and old naturalists were confident that it was effective in dispelling sadness.

In modern times the borage is now classified as a diuretic, and some herbalists use it for colds, fevers and lung complaints such as bronchitis and pneumonia.

Fig. 24 TRAVELLER'S JOY - This wild clematis plant, the only British species, appears in the months of May and June. It is found climbing over other shrubs on hedges where limestone and chalk enters the soil. It climbs by the help of its twisting leaf stalks and is well distinguished by its numerous greenish-white flowers. It received its name 'traveller's joy' from adorning the wayside where people travelled.

In the autumn, long after the green leaves have withered, the plant is more conspicuous and still beautiful with its large tufts of feathered seed vessels, when it is popularly known as 'old man's beard'.

It must be acknowledged that this graceful plant is often injurious to the hedges by strangling the shrubs and bushes it entwines.

The whole plant is very acrid in its properties and, if pressed on to the skin, will raise blisters. Farmers in former years used the stalks to bind their gates together, and boys smoked them to imitate tobacco pipes.

Fig. 25 COMMON MALLOW - There are several varieties of mallow. This one is common throughout England. In olden times, because of its young roundish fruits, children called it 'cheeses', and in some country places the plant is known as 'cheese flower'. The handsome pink flower heads are seen in clusters on waste ground from June to August. Both the wild and cultivated mallows have been useful in medicine, owing to the sticky carbohydrate mixture the plants contain. The leaves were also boiled and used by country people to treat wounds and bruises, and 'mallow tea' was a medicine taken especially by the people of Paris for coughs and colds.

It is understood that the mallows were consumed by the Romans for food, in fact most of the species have been used for many reasons throughout the world.

Fig. 26 FORGET-ME-NOT - Few flowers have been written about more than the forget-me-not. A clergyman, namely Bishop Mant, told this story: 'A lady and a knight were sitting by a riverside when the lady wished for the bright blue blossoms to braid her hair. The knight dashed into the water to gratify her wishes and gathered the flowers but, sadly, was overcome by the strength of the current.

> *'Then the blossoms blue to the bank he threw*
> *Ere he sank in the eddying tide;*
> *And "Lady, I'm gone, thine own knight true,*
> *Forget-me-not!" he cried.*
>
> *'The farewell pledge the lady caught,*
> *And hence, as legends say,*
> *The flower is a sign to awaken thought*
> *Of friends who are far away.'*

So say the poets, but one of our great botanists suggests the flower owes its name to its bright blue petals and yellow eye which, once looked upon, is never forgotten.

Fig. 27 PURPLE CLOVER - This common purple clover of the meadows forms a valuable part of the hay crop. The fragrant perfume of the flowers is attractive to the bees and consequently the long tubes of the corolla abound in honey.

The plant blooms all through summer, and because of its triple leaf it also has the name of trefoil. The leaf, in former days, was in much repute as a charm against magic, and the clover was said by old writers to be not only good for cattle, but to witches too. Happily, we of later generations are no believers in such superstition.

There are seventeen species of wild trefoil. Some are purple, some are bright yellow or white. The little yellow trefoil is very common, and although shaped like the other clovers, the heads of the flowers are not much larger than a currant.

Fig. 28 WHITE DUTCH CLOVER - The white Dutch clover and common purple clover are most valuable plants used in agriculture and, although thriving on any soil, are best grown on dry chalky land.

The Dutch clover forms excellent pasture. The flowers are white, with ovoid heads and petals sometimes tinged with pink, and very fragrant. The plant has creeping roots and resists being trampled upon.

Fig. 29 SILVERWEED -

'*And silver weed with yellow flowers,*
Half hidden by the leaf of grey,
Bloomed on the bank of that clear brook
Whose music cheered my lovely way.'

The plant is very common by roadsides and on moist meadows, and the leaves may be seen there during a greater part of the year, the flowers appearing in the months of June and July. In country places the species was known by the name of 'trailing tansy' because of the habit of its growth. Its numerous leaves are covered by silky grey hairs, giving them a silvery appearance. The conspicuous flowers are bright yellow with soft velvety petals.

The roots of the plant used to be boiled and eaten by Scottish peasants, and were eagerly devoured by pigs. It has been said that the plant was formerly gathered by ladies, steeped in buttermilk for nine days and then used to remove freckles.

Fig. 30 WOODY NIGHTSHADE or BITTERSWEET - The lurid purple blossoms of this plant and its scarlet berries would lead the botanist to conclude that poison lurked within it. It is well known to be noxious, and children are tempted by its beauty to take its fruits. Should this occur, quantities of warm water should be given and medical aid sought.

The roots of the woody nightshade have a scent similar to the potato, and the similarity in their flowers points out the relationship between the two plants. The uncooked tubers of their flowers possess, in a milder form, the narcotic properties of the tribe, but the heat which prepares the vegetable for the table removes any worries of poisoning.

Bittersweet is common throughout Europe, parts of Asia and North America. In Sweden, in former years, the peasants used to bind the straggling woody stems around their wooden canes.

Fig. 31 FOXGLOVE - 'Emblem of Cruelty and Pride'.

This stately plant, growing to a height of three to six feet, is one of the most handsome of our native wild flowers. The numerous pink/purple, sometimes white, bell-shaped flowers are arranged in the form of a tapering spike, drooping after expansion. On the inside of the bells, the flowers are beautifully speckled. The plant starts to blossom by midsummer and, although quite abundant in some areas, in others it is almost unknown. The name 'foxglove' is by some a corruption of 'folk's gloves', that is 'fairies' gloves'. The Latin name is *digitalis purpurea*. It is sometimes called 'the fingers of a glove', the Germans termed it *fingerhut*, the Dutch *vingerhood* and the French *doigts de la vienge*.

Digitalis has long been valued for its medicinal properties, for, though poisonous when administered too freely, when skilfully used it gives most important relief to the sufferer.

The dried leaf of the digitalis is listed now as an official drug in British Pharmaceuticae, but it is not recommended for domestic use and is available only on a doctor's prescription.

Fig. 32 COMMON POPPY- The large common scarlet poppy, frequently found in the cornfields, hedge banks and wayside, flowers in the month of June. Even though it is slightly narcotic in its properties, it has been used as a culinary vegetable. In England, the scarlet flowers were once collected, made into a syrup and used as an ingredient for soups, gruels and porridge. Poppy flowers are extremely fragile and on this account received the name of *rhaeas* from the Greek word 'to flow' or 'fall'. There are six wild poppies, and the genus is termed *papaver*, from the Celtic word 'papa' which signifies the pap or soft food given to infants.

John Clare calls the flowers by other familiar names:

> '*Corn poppies, that in*
> *crimson dwell,*
> *Called "headaches", from*
> *their sickly smell.*'

Wild poppies grew profusely on the battlefields of Flanders, and it was then that they became the symbol of World War I. It was believed that they represented the blood of the soldiers who lost their lives in battle.

Fig. 33 CORNFLOWER - This flower is such a brilliant blue that it finds itself a place in the borders of many cottage gardens. It grows wild in many cornfields in Europe during July and August, contrasting well with the corn poppies and the rich colour of the ears of corn. The cornflower, or blue bottle, produces a rich blue dye but, as the colour fades so quickly, it was never used by the dyers' industry. The plants of the whole genus were formerly used for healing. The ancients record that one of these flowers cured a wound that had been caused by an arrow, in the foot of one Centaur Chiron, hence its Latin name *centaurea*. In modern times, however, not one of the species is found to possess any medicinal power.

Fig. 34 BIRD'S-FOOT TREFOIL - The lush green of the summer meadow is brightened by this attractive little blossom. It has been given several local names, such as 'ladies' slipper', 'pattens-and-clogs' and 'eggs and bacon'. The flower is abundant in most parts of southern Europe, and it has been a useful ingredient to the diet among the poorer inhabitants. The seeds of our native species provide food for the birds. There are four wild varieties of the plant, one of which, the 'narrow-leaved', sown with white clover, is useful for making pasture for cattle.

Fig. 35 RESTHARROW - During the months of June, July and August the restharrow is covered profusely with pretty butterfly-shaped flowers. In barren soils, where the plant is more abundant, the thorns are numerous and its strong roots make it quite troublesome. It retards the progress of the plough, its toughness causing a great impediment to the action of the harrow, hence its name 'rest harrow'.

The plant has its uses although, in its thorny state, no animal except the donkey feeds upon it. However, on better soils it mingles with the pasture and is relished by cattle. The roots are very sweet and have a distinct flavour of liquorice. The young shoots are also sweet and succulent, and in country places they were formerly boiled and formed an agreeable dish for the table. The restharrow was also used medicinally, believed to cure delirium.

Fig. 36 GREATER BINDWEED - Although this large, pure white flower has no fragrance, it is extremely elegant in its formation. If bindweed was a rare plant, the gardener would no doubt value the species. However, its weedy aggressive tendencies were soon discovered and it was shunned as a garden plant. Gardeners would throw it out on to wasteland and waysides, where it is found in great abundance today. If a pole is placed within six inches of the young shoots, the plant will reach the pole and wind itself tightly around it. Likewise it will entwine itself around any living plant growing near it. Like others of the convolvulus tribe, the common bindweed closes its flowers before rain, but otherwise its white bells can be seen often in the moonlight. It is not generally used as a medical plant.

Fig. 37 COMMON YELLOW TOADFLAX - There are about one hundred and fifty species of toadflax. The flowers are pollinated by bumblebees and seed production is very high, being scattered far and wide by the wind and rain during the months of autumn. The sulphur-yellow and orange blossoms are raised on a stem sometimes up to two feet high. The plant grows on poor sandy and stoney soil, and prefers warm situations.

In August and September it gives a conspicuous bright yellow tint to the field of the season, the flowers resembling that of the snapdragon, except that they are spurred at the base.

Country people called the toadflax 'butter and eggs', because of the sulphur and orange flowers. The sea-green foliage has a glaucous tint and, like some others of the genus, has a resemblance to the leaves of the flax. Toadflax plants were formerly used as a lotion to beautify the skin. It was also believed that the juice could be used to poison flies.

Fig. 38 COMMON RAGWORT - Although this flower opens in July, in November it is still around when the leaves have changed their colour and the birds sing of the coming winter.

'My childhood's earliest thoughts are linked with thee,
The sight of thee calls back the robin's song,
Who from the dark old tree
Beside the door, sang clearly all day long,
And I secure in childish piety,
Listen'd as if I heard an angel sing,
With news from heaven, which he did bring
Fresh every day to my untainted ears,
When birds and flowers and I were happy peers.'

The rich golden blossoms of the ragwort are very handsome, growing on their tall stems to a height of sometimes two feet. Although an attractive showy plant, it is troublesome to pasture. Its cottony downy seeds, which are produced in great quantities, are scattered by the winds.

There are several varieties of the ragwort family, the common groundsels being two of them, these being valuable food for caged and wild birds.

Fig. 39 KNAPWEED - There are three varieties of this plant: the greater, the black and the brown-rayed, all ranging in different shades of purple blossoms and different sizes of flower heads. Generally they bloom in July and August, but an occasional flower cheers up the winter months even until Christmas. They are most commonly found growing on waste ground, barren pastures and cornfields.

The greater knapweed has the familiar name of iron-weed or knot-weed, owing to its hard oblong calyx. It has been suggested that the juice of the florets of this and the black variety could make a good ink. The brown-rayed knapweed is plentiful, mainly in the south of England and parts of Scotland. The knapweed tribe is believed to have soothed bruises and healed wounds, but more recently the roots and seeds have been used as a diuretic, and also to treat catarrh.

PART II

THE PATTERN OF THE SEASONS

Each year, around the middle of February, my friends and I would button up our winter coats, put on our thick woolly scarves and gloves, and briskly make our way through the park to the woodland. What a brilliant picture awaited us; it was quite breathtaking. The delicate snowdrops, all shining white with their pretty, green, perfumed stripes, had pushed their way through the cold dark earth and carpeted the ground.

The trees were in leaf, and the buds were opening and starting to reveal their tiny flowers. Some of the catkins were expanding, and the leaflets on the sallow willow branches were folding back, showing the tips of the fluffy white balls.

The day would be cold and we would not linger too long, but on our return journey we would stop at the stone bridge, where I would have the opportunity to pick a dog's mercury specimen for my new year's collection.

Later, coming up to Easter time, we waited eagerly to see the first daffodils. They did not disappoint us. On a sunny spring day, as we went through the park, patches of golden-yellow flowers tossed their heads to greet us. When we arrived at the wood, the words of William Wordsworth would come to mind, 'fluttering and dancing in the breeze'. In between their stately stems, nestling close to the ground, would be the palest-yellow primroses, and here and there would be the occasional patch of sweet violets making a delightful contrast to the yellows. What a stunning sight this was, with the canopy of spring trees coming to life and sitting high above the scene, completing the picture.

On the way home, coming through the park, we would notice all the rhododendron bushes now in bud.

On approaching the wood in April, we could smell the scent of the bluebells coming to meet us. When we arrived, the woodland floor would be blue with flowers. It was a joy to behold, but at the same time it would be heartbreaking to see the young children, and sometimes their parents, collecting armfuls of these beautiful flowers, only to destroy them, often before they reached home. Thankfully, this practice has now been stopped by law.

At the same time as the bluebells were blooming, the beautiful ornamental flowers of the broad-leaved ramsons (wild garlic, see fig. 1) would appear in various places in the wood. These plants would grow in large clusters, but few wild flowers have a more powerful, disagreeable odour, which could be quite unpleasant to the visitor. If some unwary footstep crushed a leaf, this attractive plant would be betrayed by its pungent smell borne afar upon the breeze.

The time arrived for us to make a special visit to see the large collection of rhododendrons in all their glory. To see these at their best, the upper level of the park was where they were always the most prolific. Almost every possible flower colour you could imagine was represented here, from the palest pink to a deep rose, from a delicate lavender to the deepest purple, with scarlet, lemon-yellow and white, sporadically distributed among them. The whole picture would look like an artist's giant paint box. The very dark green, shiny, leathery leaves made an excellent backcloth to their beauty. These rhododendron flowers stayed fresh from mid-spring to early summer, giving us plenty of time to enjoy them.

Around this part of the spring, the flowering fruit trees would be in full bloom. The various varieties of the cherry, the lovely white and pink apple blossom and many others would be flourishing in the gardens. I can remember only two trees, namely the pretty crab apple tree and a wild pear growing in our park. Unfortunately, as everyone knows, the blossom on all fruit trees is very short-lived.

The trees would now be wearing their summer foliage, their green leaves becoming darker and heavier with the bright sun glimmering through the branches. In June, the summer flowers would be showing themselves, but there would be only a few species of wild flowers growing in the wood. The ones I remember mostly were the tall upright stems of the foxgloves, standing proudly in the shade of the trees, showing off their deep-cyclamen-pink and creamy-white bells. The meadows and hedgerows, however, would be a mass of summer wild flowers growing huddled together in great abundance. These would last for the rest of summertime, giving me a wonderful chance to expand my collection of pressed and preserved wild flowers.

The year was moving on quickly now, and by the end of September most of the wild flowers had left us for another year.

On Sunday afternoons, weather permitting, in the early autumn my friends and myself would visit our wonderful wood. The trees and bushes had started to display their ripe, rich berries as the foliage was starting to change colour.

By the month of November, the leaves were falling from the trees and, as we trudged through the thick carpets of red and gold, the giant oaks would be throwing down their acorns. The horse chestnuts (see fig. 40), with their spiky green fruits, would be revealing their 'conkers' as they fell.

The boys had great fun, of course, with these, but I preferred to collect the many different varieties of fruits, berries and autumn leaves. I would take them home and make them into displays, often using them for my drawing and painting.

What lovely memories! I consider myself to have been extremely privileged to have had the opportunity to enjoy such a pleasurable environment. Every year as each season comes around, how fortunate we all are and how grateful we should be, that nature provides us with such extreme beauty of the earth - cost free!

~ FOLIAGE, FLOWERS AND FRUITS ~

Fig. 40
HORSE
CHESTNUT

Fig. 41 PUSSY WILLOW - There are at least ninety kinds of willow trees, and many are so much alike that only a skilled botanist can distinguish one species from another.

The sallows are a complex group, most of which pass as pussy willows when in flower. The illustrations show the male and female flowering branches, with ripening fruits and lance-shaped clear, green leaves.

The tree or shrub is widespread, occurring over much of Britain and Scandinavia. It is found in damp woodland, scrub or hedges, and is normally in full flower by mid-March.

The willows are not generally economically useful, although some of the species are used for making cricketbats, baskets, crates and poles, while others are simply grown for ornament and decoration.

Fig. 42 SILVER BIRCH - This is both a woodland and a garden tree, flowering in April and May and fruiting in July and August. From its graceful appearance it has been called 'the lady of the woods'. It is recognised by its smooth, silvery bark. The flowers appear before the leaves, with long, drooping male catkins and shorter female catkins.

Many uses have been found for the waterproof timber and twigs of the birch. At an early period the wood was useful for making canoes. Plywood boxes and bobbins were produced, brooms were made from the twigs, and clogs were fashioned from the wood.

The leaves of the birch are used in treating skin diseases. Birch tar oil is one of the ingredients of an ointment used for the treatment of eczema and psoriasis, and the bitter-tasting birch tea is helpful for rheumatic complaints.

Fig. 43 COMMON ELM - The elm tree has a cracked, thick bark and rough, green leaves, and bears profuse dark reddish flowers. Appearing before the foliage, these tufts of stamens open in late February. The fruits or seeds are borne in rounded membranes, shown in the illustration.

The tree occurs in woods and hedgerows. A fungal disease (Dutch elm disease) carried by the elm-bark beetle has caused widespread damage, depleting the numbers of this tree in many areas in recent years.

A decoction made from the bark of the elm is soothing and diuretic and, being slightly astringent, can be used as a lotion for skin diseases. One of the most important herbal medicines is the 'slippery-elm', especially prescribed for inflammatory bowel disease and bronchitis. Slippery elm is an American tree with similar properties to our common elm, but of higher commercial value. Slippery-elm tablets are available at most health stores.

Fig. 44 SLOE BUSH - This plant is known as blackthorn when in flower or leaf, and sloe when in fruit. The buds of the cold, white flowers appear in August and September of the previous year and bloom the following April, before the small elliptical leaves. The purple/black berries or stone fruit consist of a fleshy outer part, and a hard stony inside containing one seed. Plums and damsons are all derived from the sloe. The fruits are very acceptable to birds but not very edible to humans, although they make a pleasant-tasting jam, an excellent liquor and a spurious port wine.

The flowers are a gentle laxative but the fruits are binding. Sloe berries contain vitamin C and are used to make sloe gin. Infused in boiling water, they are known to help urinary-tract diseases, also rheumatism and gout.

Fig. 45 MAPLE - When Tennyson wrote of the common maple that would 'burn itself away', he was referring to the leaves, which change to a rich blazing colour in October. The greenish- yellow flowers are quite small, and develop into curious winged green seeds known to country people as 'keys'. These change colour as they ripen. The common maple is quite a small tree, appearing in the hedgerows as a mere bush, because it is constantly being cut and clipped. The beautifully veined wood takes a fine polish and is much used for furniture. There are many varieties of maple, including the American sugar maple which provides an excellent syrup. The syrup is regarded as a health food and can be used as a substitute for sugar. The large maple yields a considerable amount of liquor and, having a pleasant sweet taste, it has often been made into wine.

Fig. 46 COMMON HAZEL - There are fifteen species of hazel but only one is British. This small tree is native to woods and coppices in most parts of the British Isles, flowering in the late spring, when the long, drooping, yellowish, male catkins appear. Female catkins are small, budlike catkins, each holding conspicuous bright crimson styles. There are three or four of the hazel nuts together, formed from within a jagged whorl of green bracts.

The timber of this tree is used for fishing-rods and makes excellent walking-sticks. The dowsing-rod of water-diviners is usually a forked hazel twig. In former times the kernels of the nuts were said to help an old stubborn cough. Hazel nuts, cob nuts and filberts are related and are rich in protein and fatty acids. The hazel nuts are particularly rich in magnesium, potassium, copper and phosphorous and are best used as a food.

Fig. 47 COMMON ALDER - This is the only British species belonging to the alder family. It is a medium-sized deciduous tree, common near river and canal banks, and very tolerant of stagnant water. The dark green leaves are glossy and, when young, their surface is slightly sticky, hence the Latin name *alnus glutinosa*. Male catkins are long and cylindrical and are produced in mid to late spring. Female catkins are dark purple, ripening to green.
The wood is very valuable for all purposes where timber is to remain under water, such as piers. It is also used for making sabots and artificial limbs. Dyed black, the alder wood is an excellent imitation of ebony. A decoction of the bark and leaves is used as a tonic; this has astringent properties and is beneficial as a gargle for sore throats.

Fig. 48 BEECH - The beech is a tall, fine-looking deciduous tree and is almost worldwide in distribution. Having grace and nobility, it takes precedence over many other British trees. In the early spring the foliage is a fresh green, later turning darker and shiny. In the month of October the leaves change to pale yellow and in November to a rich orange-brown, giving a very beautiful appearance to the landscape. The fruit is a three-sided nut, splitting when ripe, and extremely attractive to squirrels, dormice and pigeons.

Beechwood is reddish white or light brown in colour and, being hard, strong and readily bent by steaming, it is widely used for making furniture.

Fig. 49 ASH - The ash tree is a wonderful union of grace and strength, and well merits its title 'Venus of the woods'. The roots strike deeply, so exhausting the soil that nothing can live beneath it. It is one of our longest woodland natives, growing in any soil, preferring shelter and a deep, well-drained, rich loam for perfect growth.

The flowers appear in April and May, but the leaves do not unfurl themselves until many weeks later. One seed is contained in a single flattened capsule, commonly called the 'ashen key'. The ash is one of our most handsome trees, and the tough timber is more flexible than most other woods. It is used for agricultural implements, coachwork frames and several sports goods.

When the keys are ripe, they can be stored all the year round, and in former times are said to have had medicinal values for treatment such as snake bites, jaundice and kidney stones.

Fig. 50 ELDER - The elder is a common, small, spreading tree found in hedgerows and moist places. The creamy-coloured flowers, which are arranged in a disc shape, appear in May or June and give off quite a strong scent. The fruits, which ripen in autumn, are dense clusters of small, round, deep-purple berries full of juice.

The elder, a useful remedy in modern herbal medicine, has many uses. The berries are rich in vitamin C. The wine, or juice made from the fruit, taken hot or cold, will soothe a cold. Elderflower water, when mixed with essential oil, is beneficial as a skin and eye lotion. An infusion made from the flowers and some peppermint will help relieve influenza.

Elder is a very useful plant economically. The hard wood is used for making pegs, skewers and oars and, in addition to the flowers being used medicinally, the whole plant is particularly valuable.

Fig. 51 CHESTNUTS - The sweet chestnut is a member of the mast-bearing family, which includes the oak, hornbeam, birch, beech and alder. The horse chestnut is related to the maple and sycamore. The error of thinking that the two chestnuts were related arose because of an outward resemblance in their nuts.

The sweet chestnut, a species introduced long ago from sunnier climes, is now naturalised, growing in light soils particularly in the south of England. It frequently grows in parklands, small woods and copses. The tree is long-lived. Two or three trees are known to be four-hundred-and-twenty years old and still thriving. Probably the oldest tree exceeds six hundred years.

Apparently the dried leaves of the sweet chestnut, if infused in boiling water, are beneficial for treating whooping cough and respiratory tract problems. The horse chestnut is also used in modern practice for blood circulation. The outer case of the 'conker' is poisonous.

Fig. 52 COMMON HOP - A beautiful climbing plant with vine-like leaves, growing wild in copse and hedgerow, the common hop is often an escapee from the hopfields of southern Britain. The plant is the only British species, the cultivation of which goes back at least to the eighth century. It prefers warm habitats, and a damp loamy soil rich in nitrogenous material. The hop blooms from mid to late summer and the fruits are ready for picking in September or October. The hop is commonly cultivated for the sake of its catkins, which were used to give a bitter flavour to beer.

Hops are a sedative, a tonic and have diuretic properties. The flowers contain a natural antibiotic. Country people stuff pillows with hops, which are then a remedy for promoting sleep when nothing else works.

Fig. 53 DOG ROSE - Botanists describe many species of wild roses, but as a number of these are rare and difficult to discriminate, it is thought best to give a description of only one of the common ones.

The dog rose is the common hedge rose, a flower belonging exclusively to high summer and welcomed for its delicate attractiveness and sweet perfume. It blooms in June and July, in woodland, hedgerows, and thickets and thrives on a porous soil.

The fruits of the dog rose, the hips, are extremely rich in vitamin C. They also contain provitamin A (carotene), vitamins of the B group, and vitamins K and P. The hips ripen in early autumn, and their pleasant acidity explains why they are so good for scurvy and gum disease. Rosehip syrup is especially recommended for infants and is a nutritional supplement for young children. Rosehip tea can be purchased from health stores.

Fig. 54 WILD PEAR - Found in woods and hedges in mid to late spring, growing in a loamy soil, the white flowers have red stamens and are usually clustered in groups of five. The fruit that comes from them is rough, bitter and inedible, containing a bitter compound of organic cyanide. However, the wild pear tree is an important ancestor of the luscious cultivated pear. The wild pear is a small upright tree, and its black wood is remarkably like ebony. The tree is not found further north than Yorkshire, but where it does grow it lives long.
The leaves do not contribute to healing and curing of disease, but the juice of the fruit is recommended for catarrh and skin eruptions, colitis and constipation, being rich in vitamins A, B and C.

Fig. 55 CRAB APPLE - The crab apple is a truly British plant, and it is the most important wild ancestor of the cultivated apple today.

Few flowers that grow on trees present a more beautiful sight than the clusters of fragrant wild apple blossoms, with their white petals delicately tinted with pink.

In some parts of the country, cider is made from crab apples, and crab-apple jelly, although acid, has always been a favourite country delicacy.

Before the introduction of the hop in this country, cider was much more in general use than it is now. The apple juice appears to have been a drink from olden times, probably dating back to the Anglo-Saxons.

Besides the modern uses of the apple, it was formerly employed for many others. In olden times a cosmetic was made from crab-apple pulp mixed with lard and rosewater. The old herbalist Gerard tells us that if the crab apple was held in the hand, it was considered to be effective in promoting sleep.

Fig. 56 ROWAN or MOUNTAIN ASH - When in blossom, the rowan is picturesque and attractive, and is a blaze of glory when covered with its clusters of bright red berries. Wordsworth writes:

> *'She lifts her head*
> *Decked with autumn berries that outshine*
> *Spring's richest blossoms ... the pool*
> *Glows at her feet and all the gloomy rocks*
> *Are brightened round her.'*

Birds, like the thrush and blackbird, relish the showy clusters of red berries. Soon the tree is stripped but the seeds are not wasted, for, after eating the fleshy parts of the fruit, the birds drop the seeds and so plant them over a wide area. The tree is common in woods and gardens, particularly in the north.

The creamy umbels of flowers bloom in June. They are remarkably like the elder blossom and have a similar fragrance. In ancient times the berries of the rowan tree were made into marmalade.

Fig. 57 LIME - The lime, or linden tree, is perhaps better known to town-dwellers than to country folk, for it thrives in cities and towns, often planted for ornament. It produces a soft yellowish-white wood, used in furniture and toy-making. Some of the fine wood carvings in churches and cathedrals are executed in lime wood.

In open forests, the tree grows well over a hundred feet, and has a smooth bark and spreading branches. The yellowish-green flowers are followed by clusters of greenish, round fruits. The flower clusters are attractive to bees for the honey, and cattle are also fond of them.

In former times the flowers were used to treat epilepsy and vertigo. In modern times an infusion can be made for the treatment of tension and hysteria, and is soothing for coughs and catarrh. Herbalists may prescribe it for high blood pressure and nervous tension.

Fig. 58 COMMON OAK - There are nearly five hundred kinds of oak, but only two are British natives. The leaves are of many different shapes. The common oak illustrated is the best known and deserves its title of 'Hercules of the Forest', for it stands as firm as a rock. The tree is attacked by hundreds of insects, and it is believed that over fifteen hundred species feed on the common oak. In spite of these pests, in olden times the oak tree was of great economical importance due to the durability of its timber. Before the advent of metal girders and concrete units, oak wood was used on a large scale for structural work.

The flowering time of the tree is mid to late spring. The tassels we see are the male flowers, but it is from the smaller female flowers that the acorns come. They are ready in the autumn and make good pig food.

In modern times the powdered bark of the tree has been boiled and used to check diarrhoea. A decoction is antiseptic, and has been used as a gargle to ease a sore throat.

In former times the surface of England must have been covered very largely with oak forests, as indicated in the many names of towns and villages such as Oakham and Oakley, Acton and Ackworth, 'ac' being the old English for an oak.

Fig. 59 WILD CHERRY or GEAN - When the wild cherry or gean is in bloom, it is covered with a mass of delicate cup-shaped white flowers that produce myriads of cherries. The cherries of the Kent orchards are descended from the wild cherry, which was first planted in the sixteenth century. The fruit is reddish, firm and bitter, yielding little juice, which stains the hands. When the fruit is ripe it is quickly devoured by birds.

The tree is deciduous, growing in woodland and copses. It sometimes reaches fifty feet and flowers in spring. The wood is valued for its even grain. The gean is the most common of the tree species of wild cherry, the others being the dwarf cherry and the bird cherry.

Fig. 60 WILD PLUM - The branches of the wild plum are thornless, and the fruit is oval. All the cultivated varieties of plum are believed to have originated from the blackthorn, the sloe, the bullace and the wild plum.

The illustration is of the well-known plum tree which has been cultivated in gardens and orchards for centuries. However, it is found wild, preferring to grow on the sloping ground of a hill. The flowering-time of the plum is early spring.

In former times the plum had several medicinal values. The dried leaves are used in modern times as a laxative, a diuretic and to lower the temperature in fevers. Dried plums (or prunes) are a laxative and a tonic and are eaten at breakfast for the best results.

Fig. 61 BLACKBERRY or BRAMBLE - This is an extremely common shrub, distributed widely around the country in hedgerows and copses. The plant flowers from June to late August and ripens its fruit in early September to October. The blossoms and fruit may be seen together in late summer.

The bramble climbs to a height of five to ten feet. The flower stems are fleshy and the whole plant is extremely prickly. The petals, which vary in size, are often pink but sometimes white. The berries, rich in vitamin C, are black or reddish black. They taste good and are very much used for drinks, confectionery and flavourings.

In olden days many health problems such as wounds, sores, kidney and throat troubles were treated with decoctions made from the blackberry leaves, roots and berries, and found to be effective.

Armed with bowls and basins, families have spent many happy hours on sunny summer days 'blackberrying' in the countryside. Later, everyone would be eagerly awaiting those delicious blackberry pies that mother would lovingly produce.

Fig. 62 COMMON YEW - This is the only British yew. It is an evergreen tree, very remarkable for its longevity, living for several thousand years. It grows up to thirty feet, flowering from February to June. All the green parts of the tree are highly poisonous, but the berries are said to be innocuous.

A long time ago yews were planted in churchyards and cemeteries as a symbol of mourning. The wood is tough, contains no resin, and is insect proof. It is more durable than any other European wood and was formerly used to make archers' bows.

The yew is useless for medicinal purposes, owing to its highly poisonous characteristics.

Fig. 63 HAWTHORN - The hawthorn is very common in Britain, its flowers, fruits and foliage making it easily identifiable. It is the fragrant blossom, 'the may', so called from the month in which it generally appears, that makes the hawthorn one of our favourite plants and the best of all the hedgerow trees.

The hawthorn is known by several other names, including 'may blossom', 'whitethorn' and 'quickthorn'. The flowers appear in the late spring and the berries ripen in early autumn. Sometimes, when the hawthorn grows on clay soil, the blossoms are tinged with pink. The red may flower of our gardens is a variety of the wild plant.

Birds love the fruits, and in autumn months insects find food from the leaves. The wood, when it attains a good size, is valuable for its hardness, and the hawthorn is said by agriculturalists to be the best hedge plant in Europe.

In former years, the seeds boiled in wine were supposed to relieve stomach pains. Today, a tincture made from the berries may be used by a competent herbal practitioner to treat cardiac patients.

Fig. 64 SYCAMORE - The sycamore is a large, handsome tree, growing to a height of sixty to a hundred feet. It was introduced into England in the fourteenth century and is now completely naturalised. The name 'sycamore' was given to the tree by the old botanists, who believed it to be almost identical to the 'sycomore' or mulberry fig of Palestine, which it resembles in form and foliage.

The yellowish-white wood of the tree is more prized by cabinet-makers than that of its close relation, the common maple. Sycamore timber, which is pale and long-wearing, is popular for kitchen utensils and ornamental carvings. Its pendulous panicles of greenish-yellow flowers are conspicuous in the spring, as are the clusters of winged fruits in late summer and autumn.

The sycamore grows wild in Europe and is found in woods, hedges and gardens. The whole plant is full of juice, which is taken from the tree by piercing the bark, and in former times was used in the process of healing fresh wounds. In later years the juice has been used for making wine.

Fig. 65 WALNUT - The walnut tree is found in woodland and gardens. It was introduced to this country in early times, and is common especially in the south and south-west, but less frequent in the north. At flowering time, in late spring, it produces male hanging catkins, with the female flowers in short erect spikes. The fruit is globular, green and smooth. The edible nut is formed in two corresponding sections with a hard, wrinkled shell.

The walnut timber is used for furniture-making. In early times, the green husks were boiled with honey and used as a gargle for sore mouths and inflammation of the throat and stomach. Walnuts are rich in manganese, and in recent years the leaves, infused in boiling water, have been used for complaints such as eczema and ulcers. An infusion of the powdered bark is a laxative.

Fig. 66 HOLLY -

> *'The holly and the ivy,*
> *When they are both full grown,*
> *Of all the trees that are in the wood,*
> *The holly bears the crown.'*

Holly is a corruption of 'holy', from the use to which the boughs are applied in decorating churches at Christmas. In shape, the holly tree is a pyramid, and it thrives particularly well on sandy soil. No other tree that grows wild in Britain has its foliage so protected against would-be foes. Animals are kept off by the sharp leaf spines.

The flowers of the holly are small and, being white, are inconspicuous but do make a good show in May and June. The berry or fruit is a stone fruit. Instead of having only one stone and seed inside the fleshy part, like a plum or cherry, it has four little stones, each with its own seed. In September the bright-red, glossy berries look their best, and may retain the fruit throughout the winter, for they are hard and unpalatable to small birds. Blackbirds, however, like them.

As the wood of the holly tree is very hard and almost white, it takes a fine polish, and is in great demand by cabinet-makers for veneering and inlaying.

The leaves have medicinal virtues in that they contain theobromine, which has a weak diuretic effect on the kidneys and dilates coronary arteries. The berries are poisonous, being strongly emetic and purgative, but have been used to treat dropsy, fevers and rheumatism. Chopped holly leaves infused in boiling water have been effective in the treatment of coughs, colds and influenza.

AUTHOR'S REMINDER

It cannot be expressed too strongly, that the recipes found in these pages must not be used without the advice of a professional in the practice of herbal medicine.

PART III

FROM WILD FLOWERS
TO GARDEN FLOWERS

With my family grown up and married, I retired from work in 1979 and decided at long last I could take up my art again. Having a particular interest in plants, I specialised in what I enjoyed most - flower-painting, especially in watercolour, both wild and garden varieties. I developed my own particular style and after several years of practice, culminating in many art projects and solo exhibitions, I had the urge to write and illustrate a book. My intention was to introduce just some of the great number of beautiful wild flowers; the foliage, flowers and fruit of magnificent trees; and garden flowers.

As I have always found it fascinating to learn of the practical purposes of plants, both past and present, I have endeavoured in this book to include a brief account of these uses to support my illustrations. Here I must express my indebtedness to the quaint beliefs of the early English herbalists, who have written with such real love of their subject.

In Part III we are to look at some of the more elaborate and colourful cultivated flowers that make such a spectacular show in our private gardens and public displays.

When we come to the intrigue and fascination of these flowers of the garden, we are struck by three great differences between them and the wild flowers of the countryside. In the first place, the blossoms are generally much finer and larger; in the second place, their colours and designs are much richer; and, finally, the scent is much more fragrant and powerful.

All these improvements have been brought about by the plant-breeder, who has selected those plants which have shown signs of the qualities he desired and bred from them, until he has produced these characteristics.

Let us take the rose, for example. In wild nature there is no plant that produces a double rose. All the wild roses have five petals and many stamens and several pistils. With care and coaxing, the plant-breeder has persuaded the rose to turn most of the stamens into petals and changed its colour until he has reached the result he requires. So now we have roses of almost every tint, from white to yellow and pink to darkest red - but no blue rose as yet.

The greatest plant-breeder of all time was American-born Luther Burbank. He took a Californian poppy, a flower which is generally orange but, in this rare case, had a faint line of crimson running up the centre of a petal, and from it he patiently produced a beautiful crimson, Californian poppy. From the red Shirley poppy, a blue poppy was produced. He crossed the little ox-eye daisy of the United States with a European daisy and produced a large graceful flower, and then he crossed this daisy with a dazzling, white, Japanese daisy, measuring about six inches across. From this we now have the shasta daisy.

One of the most wonderful results of the plant-breeder's work is the enormous range of colour and pattern of the pansies, which have been produced from the little wild heart's-ease of the fields. From the buttercup family have come many beautiful garden flowers, including the various forms of clematis, anemones and peonies. Thus a great number of garden flowers of all hues are constantly being born and cultivated for our pleasure, enjoyment and admiration.

~ GARDEN FLOWERS ~

Fig. 67
ANENOME

Fig. 68 SNOWDROP - The snowdrop, a member of the amaryllis (lily) family, is the sign of the awakening spring, and is frequently first seen in January.

The snowdrop flower, though growing wild, has probably escaped from gardens and multiplied in the wild state. It has a small bulb, which every year produces a scale leaf, two foliage leaves and a tall flowering stem that bears a single flower. The white flower is made up of three outer segments, large and spreading and very white, and three inner segments, which are shorter, erect, notched and greenish. The flower opens and closes according to the temperature and is fertilised by bees, which land on the outer segments, grasp the inner ones, and bring a shower of dusty pollen on their heads which they then carry to another flower. Apparently the word 'snowdrop' is derived from a sixteenth-century German word which refers to pendant ear-rings of the time. The perfume of the plant is emitted from the bright green patches seen on the inner petals.

Fig. 69 CROCUS and MEADOW SAFFRON - Crocuses are classed in two divisions, the crocus which creates a splash of colour in the early spring, and the meadow saffron of the autumn crocus which blooms in October and November. Both are hardy and flower freely from a bulb in common soil. The two species are exactly alike, except that the flowers of the meadow saffron have six stamens instead of three. These stamens are the source of the saffron which, when dried, is used as a culinary flavouring, as a medicine and as a dye. It takes over fifty thousand autumn crocus blooms to make one pound of saffron.
The genus is a member of the iris family, and it is a native of Europe and middle Asia. The saffron is chiefly grown in Spain and France, but, strangely, it is found growing wild here in Britain, in the Saffron Walden area.
The Romans once burned saffron as incense, while Arabic women used it as a cosmetic to stain their eyebrows and finger nails.

Fig. 70 DAFFODIL - Along with the snowdrop and crocus, the daffodil welcomes the spring to our gardens. I think even the non-flower-lover will recognise and greet the daffodil with affection. The nodding habit of the flower heads, bending down from their stalks, relates to the legend of the mythical youth Narcissus, who was so captured by the reflection of his beautiful features mirrored in a pool, that he was rooted to the spot, where he became changed into a flower and died.

Gerard, the old herbalist, knew this flower as 'daffodowndilly', but it was also called 'daff-lily', 'affodil', 'chalice flower' and 'lent lily'. I call them 'trumpets of joy and hope', and I never see daffodils without thinking of William Wordsworth's delightful poem 'To Daffodils'. His daffodils carpeted a meadow skirting Lake Ullswater in the Lake District, and remained to him an unfading memory.

> *'I wandered lonely as a cloud*
> *That floats on high o'er vale and hills,*
> *When all at once I saw a crowd,*
> *A host of golden daffodils,*
> *Beside the lake, beneath the trees,*
> *Fluttering and dancing in the breeze.'*

The term 'daffodils' generally refers to the members of the large narcissus family that bear trumpet-shaped blossoms. A vast number of varieties of the plant now exist and, in the language of flowers, the daffodil stands for 'chivalry'.

The plant is not recommended for domestic use. There have been cases when the bulb has been eaten in mistake for an onion, although a homeopathic medicine has been made from the bulbs, for the treatment of respiratory diseases.

Fig. 71 TULIP - The early history of the tulip is well documented and has often been retold. Tulips occur naturally in Europe, particularly Holland, but also in North Africa and central Asia. The plants appear to have been brought to Britain sometime in the sixteenth century and found to be hardy enough to flourish outdoors. They were cultivated in Turkey as early as 1561, and the name 'tulip' was derived from *tuliban*, a Turkish word meaning 'a turban'. The common garden tulip was cultivated about the same time in Constantinople and found its way here under the name 'Turkish tulip'.

A century after its introduction, the tulip became an object of commercial, profitable speculation, there being an enormous interest which reached fever pitch. At the beginning of the eighteenth century, this 'tulip mania' as it was called was at its height. Fortunes were made, bulbs selling for hundreds of pounds each. Forty years later the bottom fell out of the market, with thousands of people being financially ruined. The tulip, however, survived in Holland even when the mania settled down.

A nurseryman's catalogue today will list several hundreds of extensive varieties of the tulip, which is now one of our most showy and colourful spring blooms.

Fig. 72 FLAG IRIS - Few flowers have been more used in the decorative arts than the iris. It is found in Egyptian and Persian art, and in later medieval times it was continually used, especially in ecclesiastical work, in stone, metal and stained glass, and also incorporated in embroideries and heraldry. It is equally prominent in modern design.

There are about three hundred species of the iris plant growing in many areas of the world, but only two are native to this country. The genus is prolific in Greece, Japan, Italy, Egypt, India and especially in the Caucasus mountain range.

It is a tall, graceful flower in our gardens. In the sunlight, the bearded purple/blue blossoms portray extensive variations of the colours of the rainbow. The lower three petals or segments represent valour, wisdom and faith. Louis VII of France chose the flower on his second crusade, and the iris became *Fleur de Louis* which later became *Fleur de Luce* and finally *Fleur de Lys*.

In the British Isles, the yellow flag iris is quite abundant, skirting the margins of ponds and rivers, but the actual structure of the plant varies very little from the purple variety.

One form of iris is the source of the arris root which, when dried and powdered, becomes violet-scented and for years has been used in perfumery preparations. Many varieties of the genus have been cultivated by the old herbalists for the medicinal properties of the root.

Fig. 73 RHODODENDRON - There are about six or seven hundred varieties of this species. Plant explorers such as Sir Joseph Hooker, Robert Fortune and George Forrest have risked their lives several times to collect seeds from many eastern areas. The rhododendron is a native of China, Tibet, India, Burma and Nepal, with many of the original species coming from the mountainous regions of the Himalayas. From these sources we now have a very large number of hybrids, many of those from the Indian shrub, which has a strong scent.
The derivation of the name 'rhododendron' comes from *rhoden* (a rose) and *dendron* (a tree). The plant is an evergreen bush or shrub, growing from about five to fifteen feet, with leaves of thick, leathery texture which are dark sombre green on the upper surface and paler green or sometimes a russet colour below. The clusters of blossoms give an infinite variety of beautiful colours, flowering generally in May and June.
One of the botanical differences between the rhododendron's very close relative, the azalea, is that the former has many stamens, with the latter having only five.

Fig. 74 LILAC - The lilac is a sweet-scented, early-flowering shrub, often found in gardens or lining suburban streets. Unfortunately, it has only a short flowering-season and can often be damaged by a frost. Periodically the shrub should be pruned, otherwise it will grow tall and leggy.

The plant is cultivated throughout Europe in a variety of differently coloured, single or double flowers. Most are derived from the eastern European native 'the common lilac', introduced to this country in the sixteenth century. The blossoms come in quite a variety of colours, from pale mauve to a rich violet, a purple magenta colour and a brilliant pure white. The lilac is a member of the olive family, and the name 'lilac' comes from the Greek word *syringa*. It was in Persia that the custom originated of presenting a spray of lilac to a lover as a way of indicating that the romance had died. In the language of flowers, the lilac or syringa is also said to mean 'forsaken'.

Fig. 75 PEONY - The peony plant originated in the Far East, and it was first discovered by Abbé Delanay in China, in the province of Yunnan, during a ten-year mission there around 1887. Delanay sent the plants to Paris, but for many years they were apparently never unwrapped. Early in the twentieth century, the plant-hunter E. H. Wilson sent peony seeds back from China to Britain, along with a great number of other species. Many other plant-hunters have made expeditions to China, gaining interesting observations of peony specimens.

The popular name for the peony in China is *moutan* which means 'male vermilion'. The peony has produced very beautiful double (illustrated) and single blooms, and, strangely, is related to the wild buttercup; looking at it carefully, the single peony in particular does resemble the buttercup. Paintings of Chinese origin suggest that, hundreds of years ago, not only pink, red and white flowers were grown in China, but also yellow, dark-red and even green ones.

From early times, according to folk-lore, the peonies have had a medicinal reputation and the species was actually named after the physician Paeon. The medicinal properties are no longer acknowledged, except in Chinese medicine.

'Shame' is the symbol of the peony, the reason being that, in olden days, it was said to cure shameful diseases such as leprosy and lunacy.

Fig. 76 PANSY -

> '*Pray you love, remember,*
> *And there are pansies, that's for thoughts.*'
> Shakespeare

Pansies are sacred to St Valentine, deriving their name from the French *pensées* for thoughts or 'you occupy my thoughts', which is their symbolic meaning in the language of flowers.

In Shakespeare's *A Midsummer Night's Dream*, Oberon squeezes 'love in idleness' juice into Titania's eyes to make her fall in love with the first living creature whom she sees on waking. The pansy is still known by the name 'love in idleness' in Stratford-on-Avon, Shakespeare's birthplace. In the same play, Oberon tells the lovely story of how Cupid's love arrow missed its mark and fell on a little white pansy flower and coloured it purple. Shakespeare refers to it as 'Cupid's flower'.

There are no less than twelve other names for the pansy used in other parts of the country. Three of these are 'kiss me at the garden gate', 'jump up and kiss me' and 'three faces under a hood'. The Anglo-Saxon word seems to have been 'bonewort', which is not so poetical as the other many descriptive words the pansy has acquired.

Most pansy varieties with their attractive designs and patterns flower throughout the summer. The flower was developed from the little wild heart's-ease.

Fig. 77 POPPY - The illustration is the oriental poppy, the familiar perennial of gardens that grows from two to four feet. It has bright scarlet petals like crumpled silk, with black feathery centres. The blooms are particularly eye-catching. Their colour is so vibrant, almost garish, but although they have a brief life-span, they make a breathtaking show in spring.

The species was found growing in America and Turkey by a French botanist. He sent the seeds to Paris, and from there they were distributed to Holland and England. Until the late 1930s, scarlet was the only colour, but new varieties have been bred, with pink and white flowers now being available.

The poppy seeds are edible, but the French botanist is reported to have said that the Turks were accustomed to eating the whole green seed head as food, even though it was bitter and acrid.

I would say that flower artists make paintings of the oriental poppy more than any other species available in the spring.

The well-known opium poppy, with its white, lilac and purple flowers, comes from Greece and the Orient, and it is, perhaps, the oldest poppy in cultivation. The variety was probably introduced to England by the Romans. Although opium poppies are grown in Britain, the climate is not suitable to produce the opium drugs, morphine, codeine and heroin.

One of the best-known poppy species is the brilliant sky-blue Himalayan variety, the *meconopsis*. The flower was introduced to Britain in 1924 from western China. If the soil is right, the four-petalled *meconopsis* reaches a height of four feet and will grow well in this country.

Fig. 78 DIANTHUS - The genus is a very large one, with over four hundred species, including the popular pinks, carnations and sweet williams. The English common name given to dianthus was 'sops-in-wine', derived from the practice in Spain of adding the clove-scented flowers to wine to give it a spicy flavour. Other names came later, such as Chaucer's 'clove-gilofre', Shakespeare's 'gillvore' and later 'gilliflower'. The latter is easier and is a corruption of the Latin name meaning 'a clove'. 'Clove pinks' were used by herbalists for the treatment of nervous disorders and fevers. The order contains numerous handsome plants. Their swollen stem joints and pointed petal edges are their main characteristics, which justify their beauty and their name dianthus, which means 'divine flower'. The pink differs from the carnation, being a much smaller and hardier flower.

In medieval art, garden pinks usually signified that a lady was engaged to be married. The flower features in many paintings by the old masters, such as Van Eyck and Rembrandt.

Interestingly, the pink was not named after the colour; in fact the colour was named after the flower. The word (referring to the colour) was first used in a description in 1720; before that the colour was always described as flesh-coloured, blush or carnation.

One member of the dianthus family, the sweet william, is a good old-fashioned flower. The colours and designs are varied and fascinating. It has been suggested that the flower was named after William the Conqueror, or, possibly, from a less aggressive person, St William. Other names given to the blooms are 'London tufts' and 'velvet williams'.

Fig. 79 CLEMATIS -

'The creeper, mellowing from an Autumn bush;
And Virgin's bower, trailing airily.'

John Keats

Because of its sweet fragrance and abundance of flowers, the clematis, known also as 'the Virgin's bower', is a great favourite in English gardens. It is quite amazing that there are more species of the clematis plant distributed around the world than there are roses. The clematis was introduced mainly from China, some being discovered by the plant-hunter Robert Fortune.

Like the peony, the clematis is included in the buttercup family and, if looked at carefully, some resemblance will be observed. Many of the species are very beautiful; the variety illustrated is named 'The President'.

The wild flower, traveller's joy, illustrated and explained in Part I, is a familiar climber of the hedgerows and, like the cultivated clematis, if the plant is bruised it can cause skin ulcers and blisters. The plant represents 'artifice', because beggars and gypsies, during the reign of Elizabeth I, used to press it to their skin to cause sores, trying to attract compassion and charity.

Fig. 80 ROSE - In one form or another, and for a variety of reasons and purposes, the rose is the most famous of all garden flowers. Throughout every period of history there have been references to roses figuring as a sign of faithfulness, high regard and remembrance. Flowers are often used to express love in all its forms and to symbolise true love, but it is the rose, with its sharp thorns, beautiful colours and delicately scented flowers, which survives happiness and misfortune alike, but which speaks mostly of love.

No one can say exactly when the rose first made its entrance among flowering plants, but it is estimated to be between thirty-five and seventy million years ago. It has been discovered that the birthplace of the rose was Persia. The rose industry spread to Europe through Turkey. Its romantic associations were widely revived in the Middle Ages, and the red rose is the rose of myth and legend, adopted as the symbol of the blood of the martyrs.

Aphrodite, the goddess of love, was said to have created the red rose when she was running to comfort her lover who had been gored by a wild boar. She scratched herself on the thorns of a rose bush and her blood turned its white blossoms red.

The growing of the rose has always been surrounded by some mystique. It found its way into herbal medicine for the treatment of heart, stomach, liver and lung disease. In more modern times it has been used in perfumery in the form of skin lotions, perfumes and creams.

I have illustrated the 'Nevada' rose. This large bush displays a mass of single white flowers with blooms about four or five inches across. They present a spectacular show of real beauty.

Fig. 81 LILY - Next to the rose, the lily is considered to be the fairest of all flowers. Precisely how many species there are is difficult to discover, as they go right back to the first century and they all carry a bit of human history. Lilies are so well known and admired, it seems hardly necessary to give a description of the genus. The flowers are large and showy and are grown from a bulb. A single bulb can produce about a dozen flowers on a single stem.

Some say the name 'lily' is taken from a Celtic word for white; others believe it comes from a Greek word meaning 'a tall stately flower'.

The white lily, or Madonna lily, which Chaucer called 'Heven's lilie', is probably the oldest to be cultivated, for it is found pictured on vases and objects dating from centuries before Christ. Its purity and sweet scent made it a symbol of the Virgin Mary, and it appears in most paintings of the Annunciation. It was a symbol of elegance and purity. The flower was used by artists and sculptors in Elizabethan times, and Shakespeare mentions it constantly in his writings.

A bread made from lily bulbs has been administered for healing properties, such as the dropsy and tumours. If soaked in brandy, it is reputed to have been beneficial in the treatment of coughs and asthma.

World-wide cross pollination has resulted in a range of lovely shades of lily. The one in my painting is named 'Enchantment' from the Oregon, and is an excellent garden flower, producing many blooms from a single bulb.

Fig. 82 SWEET PEA -

> *'Here are sweet peas on tip toe for flight,*
> *With wings of gentle flush, or delicate white,*
> *And taper fingers catching at all things*
> *To bind them all about with tiny rings.'*
>
> John Keats

Sweet peas are some of my favourite flowers. I think the fragrance of the flower contributes much to their popularity. The height of the sweet pea vogue came in the Edwardian era, when it was a favourite with gentlemen for their buttonholes and also a special favourite of Queen Alexandra. The sweet pea arrived in England from southern Italy in 1699, and the seeds were generally available by 1730.

The small fragrant flowers, peculiar for their elegant shape, delicacy and richness of colouring, became steadily popular. In the beginning there were actually only five colours, but in more recent years the size, the shape and the colours have been much improved.

A man named Henry Eckford was responsible for the sweet pea business in Wen, Shropshire, where he started with five varieties. There is now, in Wen, an Eckford Sweet Pea Society, where a sweet pea show is held every year. This must be a lovely sight, displaying all the delicate pastel shades interspersed with the more recent rich darker colours.

The present Earl Spencer is following the long-standing family tradition of putting on the yearly Sweet Pea Spencer show at Althrop, Northamptonshire. For anyone who can take advantage of such an exhibition, it must be a great delight to be a spectator at this magnificent display.

Sweet peas are an emblem of lasting pleasure, because the flowers constantly renew themselves if they are cut at regular intervals.

Fig. 83 HYDRANGEA - When the hydrangea was first discovered in southern Japan, in the mid-eighteenth century, mistakes were made with regard to the flower's identity. Carl Peter Thurnburg, a Swedish doctor, thought it to be a vibernum, but by the time it was introduced to England it had become commonly known as 'the hydrangea'. To these beginnings may be traced many of the numerous distinctive breedings including the few hundred 'mop-heads' and eleven 'lace-caps' that are widely grown today.

The hydrangea gives magnificent blooms without ever producing fruit, and its name was derived from *hydor* for water and *aggeion* for a jar or vessel, because it needs a good deal of water to survive.

As the plant produces such excellent, impressive flowers, it was likened to 'a boaster', because the blooms are showy but develop into nothing of substance.

> *'No more delays, vain boaster! but begin,*
> *I prophesy beforehand I shall win:*
> *I'll teach you how to brag another time.'*
>
> John Dryden

It is commonly cultivated for its beauty, but is believed to have had medicinal uses for bladder and kidney complaints.

If the hydrangea is grown in lime rich soil, it promotes pink blossoms; if in acid soil, the colour will be blue.

Fig. 84 SUNFLOWER - Many people will immediately think of Van Gogh's famous sunflower painting, which several years ago sold at auction for millions of dollars.

Since that time, the sunflower has been very much in vogue, and has been used as an emblem for various charities and also for commercial advertising purposes.

The flower is included in the daisy family and is a native of south America and Peru. It was once the sun god of the Incas. Spanish invaders found exquisite representations of the sunflower sculptured in gold in the Inca temples.

The plant's meaning 'haughtiness' may have arisen because it can grow to a great height, giving a dominant look. The herbalist Gerard claimed he grew flowers to a height of fourteen feet, but it is said that in the royal gardens in Madrid sunflowers grew to twenty-four feet; in Padua in Italy it is reported that they have attained a height of forty feet.

The sunflower seeds make an excellent cooking oil and, when roasted like coffee beans, they can be made into a drink. The seeds, sprinkled over salads and vegetables or eaten like nuts, are a beneficial health food.

The flowers contain a yellow dye and the leaves when dried, have been used in place of tobacco.

> '... *and all tall shows*
> *That Autumn flaunteth in his bushy bowers;*
> *Where tom-tits, hanging from the drooping heads*
> *Of giant sunflowers, peck the nutty seeds.'*
>
> Robert Bridges

Fig. 85 DAHLIA - The dahlia was first grown by the Aztecs about four hundred years ago, but Spanish invaders introduced it to Europe in 1789. Its first appearance coincided with the French Revolution, but the flowers perished and were lost. The second introduction coincided with Napoleon being made Emperor of France, and it was from these incidents that the dahlia was chosen as the symbol of instability.

The genus was named after a Swedish botanist, Dr Andreas Dahl, who had great hopes that the dahlia would gain in popularity as a vegetable similar to the potato, but there was great disappointment when the tubers were rejected as unpalatable to men and cattle. Dr Dahl's expectations therefore were not fulfilled, and he died an unhappy man. In Britain, however, by the 1800s, the dahlia had become the most fashionable flower in the country. The different forms of the plant were remarkable in the diverse shapes and colours it had produced, and it now provides striking beauty in the garden until October.

Unlike many popular flowers which take several years to reach flowering stage, dahlias can be grown from seed to maturity in just one season. Garden catalogues list about a dozen species. It was discovered that the tubers contain insulin, and were therefore used in the treatment of diabetes.

Fig. 86 CHRYSANTHEMUM - When translated from the Greek, *chrysos* means 'golden' and *anthos* means 'flower', so the chrysanthemum signifies 'golden flower'. The first species happened to have yellow flowers.

The plant, long held in high regard in the Orient, was grown by the Chinese five hundred years before the birth of Christ. The Japanese held chrysanthemum exhibitions from 900 AD. This notable flower has a relatively short history in our country. The genus was not introduced to England (by Miller) until 1764, and it was cultivated at the Chelsea physic garden. In all, there are now over a hundred varieties, both single and double, widely distributed throughout the world.

When the culture of the chrysanthemum spread from China and Japan, it was made the personal emblem of the Emperor Mikado. Poems in praise of the flower were written by the Emperor himself, and the order of the chrysanthemum was the highest honour in his power to bestow. The 'rising sun' on the Japanese flag represents, not the sun, but a chrysanthemum, with a central disc and sixteen flaring petals.

Today, chrysanthemum-growing has become an industry. It used to be considered an autumn and winter flower signifying cheerfulness, because its glorious blooms brightened the dreary month of November. Now, sadly, the flowers can be bought all the year round.

> *'In the second month the peach tree blooms,*
> *But not till the ninth the chrysanthemums,*
> *So each must wait, till his own time comes.'*
>
> Old Chinese proverb

Fig. 87 POINSETTIA - The poinsettia is a member of the family of spurges, which is an immense group of around two thousand species. The poinsettia is one of the euphorbias. The vibrant bright-red bracts are not petals, as they appear to be, but are leaf-like forms. This familiar, tropical American pot plant is named after Jack R. Poinsett, an ambassador from the United States to Mexico. He brought the poinsettia from South Carolina, where it blooms in the month of December, and is therefore linked with Christmas time. It is very popular in Britain as a Christmas decoration, but in the sub-tropics it grows into a small tree.

Fig. 88 CHRISTMAS ROSE - Throughout January and, indeed, from the middle of December, flowers are at their most scarce for cutting and for house decoration; yet there are Christmas roses! The hellebores are notable for flowering early, and most of the species grow on chalk in Europe. Some plants have rather woody leaf-bearing stems, whereas others are almost stemless with a crowd of basal leaves. These include the Christmas rose *(helleborus niger)* and the Lenten rose *(helleborus orientalis)*, the latter appearing at Easter time, hence its name.

The Christmas rose is a low-growing plant and has white flowers, often lightly tinged with other soft colours. The flower turns green after fertilisation. It has five-lobed leaves, and is distinguished from the taller Lenten rose, which bears cream or purple blooms.

CONCLUSION
Inspiration from flowers

What a magnificent world of wonder and great beauty we have been born into! Mankind, the animal kingdom, trees and flowers are all interdependent on one another. For instance, have you ever considered a world without flowers? Can you imagine woods without bluebells, meadows without buttercups and daisies, avenues where no roses climb the walls? It might be worse than a sky without stars or spring without the dawn chorus.

Flowers are more varied, more elaborate and more colourful than almost any other subject available to an artist. The flower stands out as an object of almost alien beauty in our largely man-made environment.

Flowers are so much a part of our lives today that we tend to take them for granted. We grow flowers in the garden, we buy flowers to make the house look pretty, and at weddings and funerals flowers are an important part of the occasion. There are days when one is tired and depressed, and that is when a vase of flowers from a relative or friend can raise our spirits. When we receive flowers, there is no room for gloomy thoughts. They refresh our soul. When people are ill in hospital we take them a bunch of flowers, but rarely do we stop to think why, or how, these blossoms come to be an indispensable part of our lives.

In days gone by, however, flowers did have a meaning. Each flower represented something particular or carried its own special message, and this 'flower language' was generally understood. Artists knew, for instance, that lilies of the valley indicated modesty and humility, and that lilies in general were a sign of purity. Carnations, as the name suggests, were symbols of the incarnation of Christ. Paintings of the Virgin Mary often included lilies, and their meaning was understood. The rose was the Roman symbol for victory, and although the church first changed this to martyrdom, then to love, it is interesting to know that the rose once stood for something less peaceful.

Sadly, this magical language did not survive into the modern age. By the eighteenth century, flower symbolism had almost completely died out, and painters no longer sent messages to the public in the form of a bunch of flowers. They had lost their mystical meaning. The painting of flowers for its own sake has rarely been the main theme in the history of western art. We know that the Greeks and Romans decorated their homes with mosaics and frescos of flowers. There are many beautiful manuscripts surviving with decorative floral borders, but, apart from botanical drawings used to illustrate the numerous herbal books, there is little in European art that can be called flower painting. Until the advent of the great Dutch artists of the late fifteenth and sixteenth centuries, only in the East, where flower painting has been popular for more than a thousand years, did the painting of flowers enjoy artistic status in its own right. Chinese artists captured the essence and simplicity of flowers in a way which has rarely been achieved since.

More recently, flower painting has constantly brought pleasure, and artists have been seduced by flowers of natural beauty. Some painters have been inspired to use them for decorative, humorous and religious purposes, while others have made distinguished contributions to the scientific study of plants.

Painters have flourished in England, France, Germany and especially Holland, having examples of their flower art showing in many national collections. We have Pierre Joseph Redoute (1759-1841), the major creator of rose paintings executed with great skill, and masterpieces by Henri Fantin Letour (1836-1904). We have magnificent flower portraits of the Dutch artists Van Huyson (1682-1749) and Rachel Ruysch (1644-1750), and many more. Well-known examples come from the hands of the French impressionists: the flower arrangements of Edouard Manet (1832-1926), Claude Monet's (1840-1926) Water Lilies, and post-impressionist Vincent Van Gogh (1853-1890) who with great passion painted his famous Sunflowers.

Artists are still being inspired today by the styles, shapes and colours of flowers of all kinds. Flowers reflect change and continuity in the seasons of life, and it is a pleasure to be in their company. Although like the aforementioned great artists, I shall never be famous, I hope that you, my readers, have found pleasure and interest looking at my paintings and travelling with me through *A Lifetime of Flowers*.